THE BEST 50

FLAVORED OILS
AND VINEGARS

David DiResta
Joanne Foran

BRISTOL PUBLISHING ENTERPRISES
San Leandro, California

Printed in the United States of America.

ISBN 1-55867-142-0

Cover design: Frank J. Paredes
Cover photography: John A. Benson
Food stylist: Suzanne Carreiro

MIRACULOUS FLAVORS FROM A BOTTLE

Infusing oils and vinegars with marvelous, intricate flavors is uncomplicated and continues to grow in popularity. Whether you have already chartered the process, or if it is a new adventure, you'll find this collection of recipes an indispensable resource. Infused oils and vinegars can enhance salad dressings, marinades, vinaigrettes, condiments, sautés, stir-fries, roasts, stews, soups and baked goods. The possibilities are endless.

All that's required to get started is a good source for quality ingredients, a selection of basic oils and vinegars, and a few sterilized glass bottles and jars.

The flavors are intense, so use them sparingly. Let these recipes be the basis for developing your own. Use your imagination!

FLAVORED OIL INGREDIENTS

Favored ingredients infused in oils include: anise, cinnamon, cumin, coriander seeds, curry powder, cloves, basil, fennel, garlic, lemons, mint, mustard seeds, nutmeg, peppercorns, poppy seeds, oranges, oregano, sun-dried tomatoes, shiitake mushrooms and rosemary.

Since infused oils emphasize the flavors of the herbs, spices and other ingredients, use mild tasting oil varieties such as peanut, vegetable, canola or "pure" (virgin) olive oil. Generally, the rich flavor of an expensive, high quality extra virgin olive oil is not necessary. You can experiment with your own combinations of ingredients as well.

A note on olive oils

Olive oils are labeled according to their level of acidity. Pure (virgin) olive oil is the highest in acidity and has been filtered and refined. This results in a neutral-flavored oil that is well suited to infusing. For the following recipes that call for olive oil, use a pure (virgin) variety. Sometimes you can make an exception, however. For example, when making *Italian Oil* (page 24), try a first cold-pressed extra virgin olive oil (less than 1% acidity) in place of pure (virgin) olive oil. It creates an incredible dipping sauce for hot crusty bread and for brushing the top of focaccia. But for sautéing or roasting, use a pure (virgin) olive or vegetable oil.

FLAVORED VINEGAR INGREDIENTS

Some favorite ingredients infused in vinegars include: allspice, anise, basil, bay leaves, blueberries, celery seeds, chervil, chives, cinnamon, cloves, cranberries, dill, fennel, juniper berries, ginger root, garlic, lemons, mint, marjoram, nutmeg, peppercorns, tangerines, rosemary and thyme.

As in the oil mixtures, use a basic, plain tasting vinegar for infusing. White wine vinegar, red wine vinegar and champagne vinegar are good choices. Also included in this collection are a few recipes that call for rice wine, cider and balsamic vinegars; however, distilled white vinegar is not recommend because the flavor is too harsh and detracts from the clarity of the delightful vinegar mixtures.

IMPORTANT RULES TO ENSURE SAFETY AND QUALITY

- Always use top-quality ingredients. Rinse and dry all fresh herbs thoroughly.
- Make sure everything that comes into contact with the mixtures has been sterilized and is thoroughly dry.
- Use wood, glass, porcelain and plastic utensils or containers. Do not use aluminum utensils or containers. Always seal your containers with a nonmetallic cork or lid.
- Date every mixture to ensure freshness. Be sure to use them within the time frame specified in the recipe.
- Choose the smallest possible jar or bottle that will hold the ingredients. Especially in oil mixtures, extra air can be dangerous. Choose containers that will allow all ingredients to be completely submerged in the liquid. Any exposed ingredients will likely spoil.

HELPFUL HINTS

- Plan ahead. Since top quality ingredients are important, you may need to shop twice for the ingredients: once to purchase the ingredients that will steep in vinegar or oil (often for weeks at a time) and once again for the fresh herb garnishes. Infusing oils and vinegars is ideal for gardeners because of the constant supply of fresh ingredients.

- "Bruise" fresh herbs with a wooden utensil instead of cutting them. This will prevent discoloration and release more of the natural oils in the herbs.

- Blanching fresh herbs helps extract their color and flavor, and removes bitterness.

- Crush or crack spices with a spice grinder or mortar and pestle, or on a cutting board with the bottom of a heavy saucepan or skillet.

- Carefully wash citrus fruits with hot soapy water to remove the wax coating and any trace of insecticide. Rinse well.

- Use a citrus stripper or vegetable peeler to make wide strips of citrus peel. Be sure to avoid the bitter white pith. Use a citrus zester to make thread-like strips of citrus peel when you need to measure it. If you don't have a zester, remove the peel with a vegetable peeler and chop it to fit the measuring utensil.

- If a recipe calls for both the peel (zest) and juice of the citrus fruit, strip the peel first; then, juice it.

- Strain oil and vinegar mixtures through 3 to 4 layers of cheesecloth or a paper coffee filter. You may need to squeeze the cheesecloth or press down on the mixtures to release all of the oil.

HAZARDS OF GARLIC STORED IN OIL

To prevent the risk of botulism (a potentially fatal toxin that can develop in low-acidity canned or bottled foods), the Food and Drug Administration (FDA) has issued a warning to consumers that homemade mixes of garlic in oil, garlic in butter and garlic in margarine should be kept refrigerated. The FDA recommends that consumers use infused oil mixtures shortly after making them and that they refrigerate all oil mixtures and discard them immediately if they are suspected of being spoiled.

Since flavored oils are so simple to prepare, this book presents a conservative approach: prepare small batches, keep all oils refrigerated and use them within 1 week. This will ensure rich, fresh flavor without the risk of spoilage. In the case of roasted garlic oil, use it the day it's prepared. For regular garlic oil, consume it within 2 to 3 days.

FLAVORED OILS

SUN-DRIED TOMATO OIL

For a special treat, drizzle this extraordinary oil over grilled seafood, beef or poultry. It's also wonderful for dipping warm crusty breads, coating croutons and seasoning pasta salads.

½ cup dry sun-dried tomatoes (do not substitute marinated)
1 cup olive oil

Rehydrate tomatoes in boiling water for 3 to 4 minutes or according to package instructions. Drain thoroughly. Puree tomatoes and oil with a blender. Pour mixture into a sterilized glass container and cover. Refrigerate for 1 day. Oil will cloud and may congeal. Let oil sit at room temperature until it clears. Strain. Pour strained oil into a sterilized glass jar and cover tightly. Store in the refrigerator and use within 1 week.

TANGERINE OIL

For simplicity, use a gravy separator to remove the tangerine juice from the flavored oil. For a variation, you can substitute oranges. Add tangerine oil to stir-fries, salad dressings or sautéed summer vegetables and hot pasta.

peel (zest) and fruit from 2 large or 3 medium tangerines
1 cup olive oil

Chop peel and fruit into small pieces. Discard seeds. Combine oil, fruit and peel in a medium glass bowl. Cover and refrigerate for 3 to 4 hours, stirring occasionally. Strain. Use a gravy separator or carefully pour or ladle out oil floating on the mixture. Discard juice. Pour oil into a sterilized glass jar and cover tightly. Store in the refrigerator and use within 1 week.

CRACKED BLACK PEPPER OIL

Use this oil to liven up stir-fries and marinades. Shake the bottle or stir the contents before using to release more flavor. For a slightly less potent variation, substitute white peppercorns. Since it doesn't have dark black flakes, white pepper oil can accommodate pale sauces and light fish dishes.

6 tbs. whole black peppercorns
1 cup olive or canola oil

Grind peppercorns with a spice mill or mortar and pestle. Combine 5 tbs. of the pepper with oil in a small saucepan. Bring to a boil over medium-high heat, stirring frequently. Cool and strain oil mixture. Pour strained oil into a sterilized glass jar. Add remaining pepper. Cover tightly and refrigerate. Use within 1 week.

CINNAMON OIL

Cinnamon oil is extremely potent and has a familiar and distinct richness. To enhance flavor, drizzle a little oil into pancake and waffle batters, or add it to fruit pies, cakes and cookies. It goes very well with rice, potatoes and lamb dishes.

2 tbs. cinnamon
1/4 cup water
1 cup canola oil

Whisk cinnamon and water in a small bowl. Pour mixture into a sterilized glass container. Add oil and mix well. Cover and refrigerate for 1 day. Oil will cloud and may congeal. Let oil sit at room temperature until it clears. Strain. Pour strained oil into a sterilized glass jar. Cover tightly and store in the refrigerator. Use within 1 week.

ROSEMARY OIL

Use rosemary oil to enhance the flavor of grilled lamb or swordfish. It's also wonderful with roasted red-skinned potatoes, steamed asparagus and sautéed artichoke hearts.

⅓ cup fresh rosemary leaves
1 cup olive oil

Rinse and dry rosemary. Chop rosemary coarsely. Combine oil and rosemary in a small saucepan. Bring to a boil over medium-high heat, stirring frequently. Cool and slowly strain mixture. Pour strained oil into a sterilized glass jar and cover tightly. Store in the refrigerator and use within 1 week.

MUSTARD SEED OIL

Use this oil to add a robust mustard flavor and a subtle hint of rosemary to pork chops, poultry, roast beef and cold meats.

2 tbs. whole mustard seeds
1/4 cup fresh rosemary leaves
1 cup olive oil

Crush mustard seeds and set aside. Rinse and dry rosemary. Chop rosemary coarsely. Combine oil and rosemary in a small saucepan. Bring to a boil over medium-high heat, stirring frequently. Cool. Add crushed mustard seeds to oil mixture. Stir thoroughly and let mixture sit for 20 minutes. Strain. Pour strained oil into a sterilized glass jar and cover tightly. Store in the refrigerator and use within 1 week.

ANISE-POPPY SEED OIL

To add flavor and reduce cholesterol, use this oil as a substitute for melted butter in baked goods. It works exceptionally well in biscotti recipes, as well as in marinades, vinaigrettes and sautés.

1/4 cup anise seeds
1/4 cup poppy seeds
1 cup corn oil

Combine ingredients in a small saucepan. Bring to a boil over medium-high heat, stirring frequently. Cool and strain mixture. Pour strained oil into a sterilized glass jar. Cover tightly and refrigerate. Use within 1 week.

PIZZERIA OIL

This oil is wonderful as a pizza and bruschetta topping, or as a flavoring for pizza or focaccia dough. It's also marvelous with pasta or vegetables.

2 tbs. dried thyme
2 tbs. dried basil
1 tbs. dried oregano
2 tsp. crushed red pepper flakes
1 tsp. black peppercorns, crushed or coarsely ground
1 cup olive oil

Combine ingredients in a small saucepan. Bring to a boil over medium-high heat, stirring frequently. Boil for 5 seconds. Cool and strain mixture. Pour strained oil into a sterilized glass jar and cover tightly. Store in the refrigerator and use within 1 week.

SPICY CURRY OIL

Use this oil as a quick and delightful flavoring in Indian cooking.

½ tsp. curry powder
1 tbs. cumin seeds, crushed or coarsely ground
1 tbs. cardamom seeds, crushed or coarsely ground
one 2-inch cinnamon stick, crushed or coarsely ground
1 tsp. whole black or white peppercorns,
crushed or coarsely ground
1 cup corn or olive oil

Combine ingredients in a small saucepan and bring to a boil over medium-high heat, stirring frequently. Cool and strain mixture. Pour strained oil into a sterilized glass jar. Cover tightly and refrigerate. Use within 1 week.

NUTMEG OIL

This herb-spice oil blend is great for dressing up sausage, lamb and veal dishes.

1 tbs. finely grated nutmeg
5 whole cloves
1 tbs. crumbled bay leaves
1 cup olive oil

Combine ingredients in a small saucepan. Bring to a boil over medium-high heat, stirring frequently. Boil for 15 seconds. Cool and slowly strain mixture. Pour strained oil into a sterilized glass jar and cover tightly. Store in the refrigerator and use within 1 week.

OREGANO OIL

This surprisingly smooth oil is a natural choice for marinated mushrooms and olives. It goes well with sauces, soups, salads and grilled vegetables or it can be brushed on homemade rolls before baking.

1/4 cup fresh oregano leaves
1 cup olive oil
1 tsp. fresh lemon juice, optional

Rinse and dry oregano. Combine oil and oregano in a small saucepan. Bring to a boil over medium-high heat, stirring frequently. Cool and slowly strain mixture. Pour strained oil into a sterilized glass jar. Mix in lemon juice, if using, and cover tightly. Store in the refrigerator and use within 1 week.

FENNEL SEED OIL

This spicy and distinctive licorice-flavored oil will enhance the taste of baked fish, pork and cold salads.

3 tbs. fennel seeds
1 tbs. cumin seeds
1 tbs. whole black peppercorns
1 cup olive oil

Crush fennel and cumin seeds. Coarsely grind or crush peppercorns. Combine all ingredients in a small saucepan. Bring to a boil over medium-high heat, stirring frequently. Cool and strain mixture. Pour strained oil into a sterilized glass jar and cover tightly. Store in the refrigerator and use within 1 week.

LEMON AND THYME OIL

This classic combination works exceptionally well with sea-food, poultry, eggs, potatoes and mushrooms.

peel (zest) from 1 lemon
1½ cups fresh thyme leaves and stems
1 cup olive oil

Chop lemon peel into small pieces and set aside. Rinse thyme. Immerse thyme in boiling water for 5 seconds in cheesecloth or a fine mesh strainer. Quickly drain thyme and plunge into ice water. Drain thyme, remove from cheesecloth and dry thoroughly. Puree all ingredients with a blender. Strain. Pour strained oil into a sterilized glass jar and cover tightly. Store in the refrigerator and use within 1 week.

SHIITAKE MUSHROOM OIL

This oil is a perfect addition to quick sautés and marinades. Try it drizzled over fresh tomato slices, roasted peppers and baked eggplant. Dried shiitakes are available in specialty food stores, Asian markets and in the produce section of some supermarkets.

1/2 tsp. whole white peppercorns
3/4 -1 oz. dried shiitake mushrooms, finely chopped
1 cup olive oil

Grind or crush peppercorns with a spice grinder or mortar and pestle. Combine pepper, mushrooms and oil in a small saucepan and heat over medium-high heat. Boil for 1 minute, stirring frequently. Cool for 5 minutes and strain. Pour strained oil into a sterilized glass jar and cover tightly. Store in the refrigerator and use within 1 week.

ITALIAN OIL

This all-purpose oil is great on pizza, fish, vegetables, pasta, salads and sautés. For optimum flavor, use fresh jars of dried herbs instead of the old ones in the pantry. Or, buy them in bulk.

1 tbs. dried oregano
1 tbs. dried marjoram
2 whole bay leaves
3 tbs. dried basil
1 tsp. dried thyme

1 tsp. whole black
  peppercorns, crushed or
  coarsely ground
1 cup olive oil

Combine all ingredients in a small saucepan. Bring to a boil over medium-high heat, stirring frequently. Boil for 15 seconds. Cool and slowly strain mixture. Pour strained oil into a sterilized glass jar and cover tightly. Refrigerate and use within 1 week.

CHIVE AND LEMON OIL

This charming oil adds a delicate onion flavor to soups, sauces, vegetables and pasta dishes. It also creates a nice dressing for cold meats.

1 bunch (2 oz.) fresh chives
peel (zest) from 1 lemon
1 cup olive oil

Rinse chives; then, immerse in boiling water for 10 seconds. Quickly plunge chives into ice water. Dry thoroughly. Puree all ingredients with a blender. Pour oil mixture into a sterilized glass container. Cover and refrigerate for 1 hour. Oil will cloud and may congeal. Let oil sit at room temperature until it clears. Strain. Pour strained oil into a sterilized glass jar and cover tightly. Store in the refrigerator and use within 4 to 5 days.

ROASTED GARLIC OIL

Roasting garlic gives it a sweet, nutty flavor that goes well with mashed potatoes, pizza, baked fish, focaccia, crusty bread and pasta.

6 large garlic bulbs
1/2 tsp. dried basil
1/2 tsp. dried thyme
1/8 tsp. ground pepper
1 cup plus 1 tbs. olive oil

Cut a 1/4-inch slice from the top of each garlic bulb. Remove loose outer leaves (bulbs should remain intact). Place garlic bulbs in a deep-sided baking dish. Sprinkle with basil, thyme, pepper and 1 tbs. of the oil. Cover baking dish and bake in a preheated

350°oven for 50 minutes. Remove cover and bake for an additional 20 minutes. Cool. Separate cloves and squeeze out garlic. Discard skins. In a medium bowl, combine remaining oil and garlic paste. Mix well. Refrigerate for 2 to 3 hours. Strain. Pour strained oil into a sterilized glass jar.

CAUTION: Roasted garlic cloves and paste are very perishable. They should always be coated with oil, stored in the refrigerator and used the very same day!

GARLIC OIL

This special oil adds a savory and robust flavor to any dish, before or after cooking. Use only fresh whole garlic cloves without blemishes, yellow spots, mold or sprouts.

6 cloves garlic, peeled
½ cup distilled white vinegar
1 cup olive oil

Slice garlic cloves in half. Combine garlic and vinegar in a small bowl. Refrigerate mixture for 1 day. Discard vinegar. Mince garlic or squeeze through a garlic press. Mix garlic and oil in a bowl. Refrigerate for 3 to 4 hours. Strain. Pour strained oil into a sterilized glass jar. Cover, refrigerate and use within 2 to 3 days.

STIR-FRY OIL

Use this oil as a base for stir-fries and as a flavoring for chilled noodle dishes. Experiment with the quantity of peppercorns according to how spicy you enjoy your dishes.

1/3 cup chopped ginger root
1 tsp. dried lemon peel
2 tsp. black peppercorns, crushed
1 tsp. Szechwan peppercorns, crushed
1 cup canola oil

Combine all ingredients in a small saucepan. Bring to a boil over medium-high heat, stirring frequently. Boil for 1 minute. Cool and slowly strain mixture. Pour strained oil into a sterilized glass jar and cover tightly. Store in the refrigerator and use within 1 week.

ORANGE TARRAGON OIL

This oil boasts a mild anise flavor and a smooth citrus finish. It's quite versatile and goes well with mayonnaise, omelets, cream sauces, grilled seafood, baked chicken, beans and vinaigrettes.

1½ cups fresh tarragon leaves and stems
peel (zest) and fruit from 1 large orange
1 cup olive oil

Rinse tarragon; then, immerse in boiling water for 10 seconds. Quickly drain tarragon and plunge into ice water. Dry thoroughly. Chop fruit and peel into small pieces. Discard seeds. Combine tarragon, oil, chopped orange and orange peel in a medium bowl. Cover and refrigerate for 3 to 4 hours. Oil will cloud and may congeal. Let oil sit at room temperature until it clears. Strain. Use a gravy separator or carefully pour or ladle out the oil floating on the surface of the mixture. Discard juice. Pour strained oil into a sterilized glass jar and cover tightly. Store in the refrigerator and use within 1 week.

VANILLA OIL

Mix vanilla oil with balsamic or white wine vinegar for a truly outstanding salad dressing. It also adds a pleasing flavor to chicken dishes. There is no need to remove the vanilla bean from the oil, but be sure to keep it submerged. When the oil is gone, use the vanilla bean to flavor custards, ice cream or other desserts.

1 vanilla bean
olive oil (enough to cover vanilla bean)

Slice vanilla bean lengthwise through the center. Place vanilla bean in a sterilized glass jar and completely cover with olive oil. Cover jar and refrigerate for 1 week before using. Oil will cloud and may congeal. Before using, let oil sit at room temperature until it clears. Store oil in the refrigerator and use within 2 to 3 weeks.

HOT PEPPER OIL

Use this spicy oil to liven up sautés, marinades or vinaigrettes. Crush or coarsely grind the peppercorns with a mortar and pestle or spice grinder to release their flavor. Chiles de arbol are a good choice for the dried chiles.

6 small dried chile peppers, finely chopped
1/4 tsp. crushed red pepper flakes
1/3 tsp. whole black peppercorns, crushed
1 cup olive oil

Bring all ingredients to a boil in a small saucepan over medium-high heat, stirring constantly. Boil for 5 seconds. Cool and strain. Pour strained oil into a sterilized glass jar and cover tightly. Store in the refrigerator and use within 1 week.

LEMON-LIME MINT OIL

Spearmint and apple mint or a combination of the two are the best choices for this strongly flavored oil. It is particularly good with lamb, tomatoes, cucumbers and summer squash.

1 cup fresh mint leaves
1 tbs. chopped fresh lemon peel (zest)
1 tbs. chopped fresh lime peel (zest)
1 tsp. fresh lemon juice
1 tsp. fresh lime juice
1 cup olive oil

Rinse mint under cold running water. Immerse mint in boiling water for 20 seconds. Quickly drain and plunge into ice water. Dry mint thoroughly. Combine all ingredients in a blender and puree. Pour oil mixture into a glass container and refrigerate for 1 day. Oil will cloud and may congeal. Let oil sit at room temperature until it clears. Strain. Pour strained oil into a sterilized glass jar. Cover tightly and store in the refrigerator. Use within 1 week.

ASIAN OIL

Use this oil to add Far East flavor to roast duck, pork, fish and vegetable dishes.

1 tbs. black peppercorns
1 tbs. coriander seeds
½ cup chopped ginger root
1 tbs. anise seeds
1 cup peanut oil

Coarsely grind peppercorns and coriander seeds. Combine all ingredients in a small saucepan. Bring to a boil over medium-high heat, stirring frequently. Boil for 1 minute. Cool and strain. Pour strained oil into a sterilized glass jar and cover tightly. Store in the refrigerator and use within 1 week.

PAPRIKA OIL

This is a perfect seasoning for fish, soups, stews, chicken, eggs and pepper dishes. For best results, use sweet Hungarian paprika.

2 tbs. plus 1 tsp. paprika
1/4 cup water
1 cup canola or olive oil

Whisk paprika and water in a small bowl. Pour mixture into a sterilized glass jar. Add oil and mix well. Cover and refrigerate for 1 to 2 days, shaking or stirring contents occasionally. Oil will cloud and may congeal. Let oil sit at room temperature until it clears. Strain. Pour strained oil into a sterilized glass jar. Cover tightly and store in the refrigerator. Use within 2 months.

BASIL OIL

Drizzle basil oil over homemade pizza, or add it to the dough mixture for an adventurous and tasty crust. You can use basil oil in just about any recipe that calls for olive oil.

½ cup fresh basil leaves, firmly packed
1 cup olive oil

Rinse basil under cold running water. Immerse in boiling water for 20 seconds. Quickly plunge into ice water. Dry thoroughly. Puree basil and oil with a blender. Pour mixture into a sterilized glass container. Cover and refrigerate for 1 day. Oil will cloud and may congeal. Let oil sit at room temperature until it clears. Strain. Pour strained oil into a sterilized glass jar. Cover tightly and refrigerate. Use within 1 week.

FLAVORED VINEGARS

HOT CHILE PEPPER AND CILANTRO VINEGAR

Add this vinegar to any salsa recipe or drizzle small amounts over grilled swordfish or charred shrimp. Cilantro is also called fresh coriander and Chinese parsley. Chiles de arbol work well for the dried chiles.

3/4 cup cilantro leaves
4-6 small dried chile peppers
peel (zest) and juice of 1 lime
1 cup white wine vinegar
1 sprig cilantro

Rinse and dry cilantro leaves. Crush cilantro leaves with a
wooden utensil. Place cilantro, chile peppers, lime peel and juice
in a sterilized glass container. Cover with vinegar. Shake or stir well
and seal container tightly. Place container in a cool, dark place or
in the refrigerator for 7 days. Strain. Place cilantro sprig in a
sterilized container. Add strained vinegar. Seal container tightly
and store in a cool dark place for up to 2 months.

MINT VINEGAR

Mint, coriander and cinnamon combine beautifully in this flavored vinegar and will add a delicate citrus note and bold mint sensation to your recipes. It's perfect for fruit salad dressings, vegetables, vinaigrettes, marinades, condiments, and rice, game and lamb dishes.

½ cup fresh mint leaves
1 tsp. coriander seeds, crushed
four 1-inch cinnamon sticks
1 cup white wine vinegar or champagne vinegar
1 sprig fresh mint

Rinse and dry mint leaves. Bruise or pound mint leaves with a wooden utensil. Place mint leaves, coriander and cinnamon in a sterilized glass container. Add vinegar and seal container tightly. Place container in a cool, dark place for 2 weeks. Strain. Place clean, dry mint sprig in a sterilized glass container. Add strained vinegar. Seal container tightly and store in a cool, dark place. Use within 4 months.

RED RASPBERRY VINEGAR

Champagne vinegar has a smooth, subtle flavor that blends beautifully with the delicate taste of fresh red raspberries. This is excellent in a vinaigrette tossed with cold pasta salad or a fresh garden salad.

½ cup fresh red raspberries
1 tbs. sugar
1 cup champagne vinegar
two ½-inch-x-3-inch strips lemon peel (zest)
2 whole cloves
one 2-inch cinnamon stick
5 fresh red raspberries

Rinse and dry raspberries. Combine sugar and vinegar in a sterilized glass container and shake or stir with a wooden utensil to dissolve sugar. Add ½ cup raspberries, lemon peel, cloves and cinnamon to container. Seal container tightly with a nonmetallic cover. Place container in a cool, dark place or in the refrigerator for 1 week. Strain. Add 5 fresh raspberries and strained vinegar to a sterilized container. Seal container tightly and store in a cool, dark place. Use within 4 months.

BLUEBERRY BASIL VINEGAR

This vinegar adds a distinctive flavor to vinaigrettes and marinades. It's also delicious drizzled over steamed vegetables and fresh fruit.

12 fresh basil leaves
¾ cup fresh blueberries
1 cup champagne vinegar

Rinse and dry basil and blueberries. Bruise basil and crush blueberries with a wooden utensil. Place basil and blueberries in a sterilized glass container. Add vinegar and seal container tightly. Place container in a cool dark place or the refrigerator for 7 days. Strain. Pour strained vinegar into a sterilized container. Seal container tightly and store in a cool dark place. Use within 4 months.

GINGER VINEGAR

This blended vinegar is a great alternative to plain rice vinegar in stir-fry dishes, salad dressings and sauces. An easy way to peel ginger root is to scrape off the skin with the edge of a small spoon.

1-inch slice ginger root
$1/8$ tsp. celery seeds
$1/2$ tsp. Szechwan peppercorns, coarsely cracked
1 cup rice wine vinegar (do not use seasoned)

Peel and chop ginger into small pieces. Place ginger, celery seeds and peppercorns in a sterilized glass container. Add vinegar. Seal container tightly and place in a cool, dark place for 3 weeks. Strain. Pour strained vinegar into a sterilized glass container. Seal container tightly and store in a cool, dark place. Use within 2 months.

CHILE PEPPER AND CHIVE VINEGAR

This vinegar's intensity varies from mild to very hot depending on the chile pepper. Jalapeños or serranos work very well. Use the vinegar sparingly in salsas, soups, salads and sautés.

4-6 fresh chile peppers (do not substitute dried)
8-10 fresh chives, about 5-6 inches long
1-2 cups white wine vinegar

Rinse and dry chile peppers and chives. Place chile peppers and chives in a sterilized glass container. Add vinegar and seal container tightly. Place container in a cool, dark place for 2 weeks, shaking occasionally. Strain. Pour strained vinegar into a sterilized glass container. Seal container tightly and use within 2 months.

FINES HERBES VINEGAR

This vinegar features a traditional herb blend that is commonly used to flavor egg dishes, fish, chicken and vegetables.

2 tbs. fresh chervil	1 tbs. snipped fresh chives
2 tbs. chopped fresh parsley	1 cup white wine vinegar
2 tbs. chopped fresh tarragon	1 chive with flower, optional

Rinse and dry chervil, parsley, tarragon and snipped chives. Bruise with a wooden utensil. Place bruised herbs in a sterilized glass container. Add vinegar and seal tightly. Place container in a cool, dark place for 2 weeks. Strain. Place chive with flower, if using, in a sterilized glass container. Add strained vinegar. Seal container tightly and store in a cool, dark place. Use within 4 months.

ITALIAN GARDEN VINEGAR

Use this vinegar to lend a savory and robust flavor to tomato sauces, sautéed vegetables, pasta dishes, antipastos and salads. Use it liberally. It makes a wonderful gift.

2 tbs. fresh oregano leaves
12 leaves fresh basil
2 tbs. fresh marjoram leaves
2 sprigs fresh thyme
2 sprigs fresh rosemary
2 dried bay leaves
1 cup white wine vinegar

Rinse and dry fresh herbs. Bruise oregano, basil, marjoram and one sprig each of the thyme and rosemary with a wooden utensil. Place bruised herbs and dried bay leaves in a sterilized glass container. Add vinegar. Seal container tightly with a nonmetallic seal. Place container in a cool, dark place for 3 weeks. Strain. Pour strained vinegar into a sterilized glass container. Add remaining sprigs of thyme and rosemary. Seal container tightly with a non-metallic seal and store in a cool, dark place. Use within 2 months.

SWEET JUNIPER BERRY VINEGAR

This vinegar is very aromatic and has an intriguing flavor that goes nicely in poultry, pork or lamb marinades. It's also great added to meat stews and stuffings. You'll find dried juniper berries in the spice section of your supermarket.

1 tsp. dried juniper berries
1 tsp. whole black peppercorns
1 tsp. whole allspice
one 3-inch cinnamon stick
1 cup red wine vinegar

Crush juniper berries with a mortar and pestle or spice grinder. Place juniper berries, peppercorns, allspice and cinnamon in a sterilized glass container. Add vinegar. Seal container tightly with a nonmetallic seal. Place in a cool, dark place for 3 weeks. Strain. Pour strained vinegar into a sterilized glass container. Seal container tightly with a nonmetallic seal and store in a cool, dark place. Use within 4 months.

DILL VINEGAR

Dried dill seeds and fresh dill leaves go particularly well together in this versatile infused vinegar. The mildly sweet, aromatic combination has a subtle licorice flavor and can be used extensively in just about any recipe. It's especially good with fish and vegetables, and tastes delicious in dips.

¼ cup fresh dill leaves
¾ tsp. dill seeds
1 cup white wine vinegar or champagne vinegar
1 sprig fresh dill, optional

Rinse and dry dill leaves. Bruise dill leaves with a wooden utensil. Place dill leaves and dill seed in a sterilized glass container. Add vinegar. Seal container tightly with a nonmetallic seal. Place container in a cool, dark place for 2 weeks. Strain. Place clean, dry dill sprig, if using, in a sterilized glass container. Add strained vinegar. Seal container tightly with a nonmetallic seal and store in a cool, dark place. Use within 4 months.

FRUIT VINEGAR

This vinegar has a subtle, yet distinctive, hint of citrus. To increase the intensity, double the quantity of citrus peel. Substitute orange peel when you can't find tangerines.

5-6 medium strawberries
1-inch slice ginger root
two ½-inch-x-3-inch strips lemon peel (zest)
two ½-inch-x-3-inch strips lime peel (zest)
two ½-inch-x-3-inch strips tangerine peel (zest)
1 cup white wine vinegar or champagne vinegar

Wash and dry strawberries. Slice strawberries into ¼-inch slices. Peel ginger and chop coarsely. Place strawberries, ginger root and citrus strips in a sterilized glass container. Add vinegar. Seal container tightly with a nonmetallic seal. Place container in a cool, dark place or in the refrigerator for 1 to 2 weeks. Strain. Pour strained vinegar into a sterilized glass container. Seal container tightly with a nonmetallic seal and store in a cool, dark place. Use within 2 months.

SPICED VINEGAR

The aromas of cinnamon and cloves in this luscious vinegar will add an outstanding flair to rich fruit dishes and pickled fish.

1 tbs. whole cloves
1 tsp. whole allspice
one 3-inch cinnamon stick
$\frac{1}{2}$ tsp. anise seeds
1 cup red wine vinegar

Place spices in a sterilized glass container. Add vinegar. Seal container tightly with a nonmetallic seal. Place container in a cool, dark place for 2 weeks. Strain. Pour strained vinegar into a sterilized glass container. Seal container tightly with a nonmetallic seal and store in a cool, dark place. Use within 4 months.

GARLIC VINEGAR

Garlic vinegar is the secret ingredient in a variety of sensational salad dressings, sauces and marinades. Make this vinegar in small batches since the garlic flavor weakens after 3 to 4 weeks. For a variation, add a fresh sprig of rosemary or oregano before storing.

2 cloves garlic
1 cup white or red wine vinegar

Mince garlic or squeeze through a press. Place garlic in a sterilized glass container. Add vinegar. Seal container tightly with a nonmetallic seal. Place container in the refrigerator for 1 week. Strain. Pour strained vinegar into a sterilized glass container. Seal container tightly with a nonmetallic seal. Store in the refrigerator and use within 3 weeks.

PINEAPPLE AND CILANTRO VINEGAR

To enhance flavors, use this vinegar in any Asian-style recipe that calls for rice vinegar.

1/4 cup cilantro leaves
1/2 cup fresh pineapple chunks
1 cup rice wine vinegar (do not use seasoned)

Rinse and dry cilantro. Bruise cilantro with a wooden utensil. Place cilantro and pineapple in a sterilized glass container. Add vinegar. Seal container tightly with a nonmetallic seal. Place container in the refrigerator for 7 days. Strain. Pour strained vinegar into a sterilized glass container. Seal container tightly and store in a cool, dark place or in the refrigerator for up to 2 months.

BASIL VINEGAR

Lemon peel freezes very well, so you'll have lots on hand whenever you need to make a new batch of basil vinegar.

1/4 cup fresh basil leaves
two 1/2-inch-x-3-inch strips lemon peel (zest)
1 cup white or red wine vinegar
1 small sprig fresh basil

Rinse and dry basil leaves. Bruise basil leaves with a wooden utensil. Place basil leaves and lemon peel in a sterilized container. Add vinegar and seal container tightly. Place container in a cool, dark place or in the refrigerator for 1 week. Strain. Place basil sprig in a sterilized container. Add strained vinegar. Seal container tightly. Store in a cool, dark place. Use within 4 months.

ROYAL PEPPERCORN BLEND VINEGAR

Allspice blends well with pepper and adds a pleasant flavor to this vinegar, but it can be omitted. If desired, you can substitute 3 tbs. of the peppercorn blend found in specialty stores.

1 tsp. whole black peppercorns, cracked
1 tsp. whole white peppercorns, cracked
1 tsp. whole pink peppercorns, cracked
1/2 tsp. whole allspice, cracked
1 cup red or white wine vinegar

Place spices in a sterilized glass container. Add vinegar. Seal container tightly with a nonmetallic seal. Place in a cool, dark place for 3 to 5 weeks. Strain. Pour strained vinegar into a sterilized glass container. Seal container tightly with a nonmetallic seal and store in a cool, dark place. Use within 4 months.

TARRAGON VINEGAR

This anise-scented vinegar adds a refined touch to mayonnaise sauces, mustards and vinaigrettes. It also imparts a nice flavor to cold bean or pasta salads.

4 sprigs fresh tarragon
1 tsp. fresh dill leaves
¼ tsp. whole black peppercorns
1 cup white wine vinegar

Rinse and dry herbs. Bruise all herbs except 1 sprig of the tarragon. Place bruised herbs and peppercorns in a sterilized container. Add vinegar and seal container tightly. Place container in a cool, dark place for 3 weeks. Strain. Place remaining tarragon sprig in a sterilized container. Add vinegar, seal container tightly and store in a cool, dark place. Use within 4 months.

ORANGE ROSEMARY VINEGAR

Clear glass bottles with porcelain stoppers and airtight rubber gaskets are ideal for storing flavored vinegars. The bottle can be easily decorated with handsome ribbons for creative gift-giving. Be sure, however, to include for the recipient the date on which the vinegar was made, written instructions and a list of all ingredients.

3 sprigs fresh rosemary
two ½-inch-x-3-inch strips orange peel (zest)
1 tsp. whole black peppercorns
1 cup red wine vinegar

Rinse and dry rosemary. Bruise 2 sprigs of the rosemary with a wooden utensil. Place bruised rosemary, orange peel and ½ tsp. of the peppercorns in a sterilized glass container. Add vinegar. Seal container tightly with a nonmetallic seal. Place container in a cool, dark place or in the refrigerator for 2 weeks. Strain. Add remaining rosemary sprig, remaining peppercorns and strained vinegar to a sterilized glass container. Seal container tightly and store in a cool, dark place. Use within 4 months.

MINTY LEMON BALSAMIC VINEGAR

For an interesting twist on a fruit salad, sprinkle this zesty fruit-flavored vinegar over fresh strawberries and kiwi slices.

⅔ cup fresh mint leaves
peel (zest) of 2 lemons, cut into ½-inch wide strips
1 cup balsamic vinegar

Rinse and dry mint. Bruise mint with a wooden utensil. Place lemon peel and mint into a sterilized glass container. Add vinegar. Seal container tightly with a nonmetallic seal. Place container in a cool, dark place for 4 days. Strain. Pour strained vinegar into a sterilized glass container. Seal container tightly and store in a cool, dark place. Use within 4 months.

FENNEL VINEGAR

Fennel has a comforting smell and taste of anise. It is excellent with vegetables, salads, pork, veal and seafood.

2 tbs. fresh fennel leaves
2 tsp. fennel seeds
1/2 tsp. crushed red pepper
   flakes

1 tsp. black or white
   peppercorns
1 cup red wine vinegar

Rinse and dry fennel leaves. Bruise fennel leaves with a wooden utensil. Place fennel leaves, fennel seeds, red pepper flakes and whole peppercorns in a sterilized glass container. Add vinegar. Seal container tightly with a nonmetallic seal. Place container in a cool, dark place for 2 weeks. Strain. Pour strained vinegar into a sterilized glass container. Seal container tightly with a nonmetallic seal and store in a cool, dark place. Use within 4 months.

PEPPERY HERB VINEGAR

The herbs and spices in this vinegar are easy to find and are available throughout the year. The flavors blend beautifully with extra virgin olive oil for marinades, tomato-based sauces, salad dressings, bruschetta and pizza toppings.

1 tsp. dried basil
1/4 tsp. dried oregano
1 tsp. dried thyme
1/2 tsp. dried marjoram
1 tsp. whole black peppercorns
1 tsp. whole white peppercorns
1 cup red wine vinegar

Place herbs and spices in a sterilized glass container. Add vinegar and shake or stir well. Seal container tightly with a non-metallic seal. Place container in a cool, dark place for 3 weeks. Strain. Pour strained vinegar into a sterilized glass container. Seal container tightly and store in a cool, dark place. Use within 4 months.

PEACH VINEGAR

Treat yourself to a splash of this fragrant vinegar over a chilled roasted chicken salad for a truly refreshing flavor. You can also use it in fish, poultry and meat marinades and over any assortment of fresh vegetables and fruits.

1 ripe peach
1 whole nutmeg, grated
one 2-inch cinnamon stick
4-5 cardamom seeds
½ tsp. whole cloves
1 cup champagne vinegar or apple cider vinegar

Wash and dry peach. Do not peel. Slice peach into thin wedges and discard pit. Place peach wedges, nutmeg, cinnamon, cardamom and cloves in a sterilized glass container. Add vinegar. Seal container tightly with a nonmetallic seal. Place container in the refrigerator for 4 days. Strain. Pour strained vinegar into a sterilized glass container. Seal container tightly and store in a cool, dark place. Use within 2 months.

LEMONY THYME VINEGAR

Thyme is a perennial herb plant that is very easy to grow in a sunny window or in an outdoor herb garden. There are several varieties to choose from including golden, silver and the popular lemon thyme.

2 tbs. fresh thyme leaves and stems
1 tsp. poppy seeds
two ½-inch-x-3-inch strips lemon peel (zest)
1 cup white wine vinegar
1 sprig fresh thyme, optional

Rinse and dry thyme. Bruise or pound thyme leaves and stems with a wooden utensil. Place thyme leaves and stems, poppy seeds and lemon peel in a sterilized glass container. Add vinegar. Seal container tightly with a nonmetallic seal. Place container in a cool, dark place or in the refrigerator for 1 week. Strain. Place thyme sprig, if using, in a sterilized glass container. Add strained vinegar. Seal container tightly with a nonmetallic seal and store in a cool, dark place. Use within 4 months.

CRANBERRY VINEGAR

Let your imagination run wild with this tangy combination. Highlight your favorite dishes with a new and exciting flavor.

1 cup fresh cranberries
two ½-inch-x-3-inch strips orange peel (zest)
1 cup white wine or champagne vinegar

Rinse and dry cranberries. Place cranberries and orange peel in a sterilized glass container. Cover with vinegar. Seal container tightly with a nonmetallic seal. Place container in a cool, dark place or the refrigerator for 5 to 7 days. Strain. Pour strained vinegar into a sterilized glass container. Seal container with a nonmetallic seal and store in a cool, dark place. Use within 2 months.

ROSEMARY VINEGAR

Fresh rosemary has a strong, distinctive fragrance, and it produces an exceptionally potent vinegar. Use this vinegar sparingly in vinaigrettes, dressings, soups, stews, sautés and meat dishes.

1 cup fresh rosemary leaves
1 cup red wine vinegar
1 sprig fresh rosemary

Rinse and dry rosemary leaves. Chop leaves into small pieces and place in a sterilized container. Add vinegar and seal container tightly. Place container in a cool, dark place for 2 weeks. Strain. Place clean, dry rosemary sprig into a sterilized glass container. Add vinegar. Seal container tightly and store in a cool, dark place. Use within 4 months.

INDEX